CW01483617

MYSTERIOUS ASCENSION

THE STRANGE CASE OF VALIANT THOR

MYSTERIOUS ASCENSION

THE STRANGE CASE OF VALIANT THOR

GRAY BARKER

NEW SAUCERIAN BOOKS, POINT PLEASANT, WEST VIRGINIA

They Knew Too Much About Flying Saucers

A Saucerian Review of Flying Saucers

Gray Barker's Book of Saucers

Gray Barker's Book of Adamski

Gray Barker at Giant Rock

The Ghost of the Philadelphia Experiment Returns

The Silver Bridge: The Classic Mothman Tale

Men in Black: The Secret Terror Among Us

Selected For Abduction

Bigfoot Shootout!

Time-Traveling Through Swamp Gas

When Men in Black Attack

Serpents of Fire

Saucers of Fear

Saucers of Fire

The Strange Case of Valiant Thor

ISBN-13: 978-1535582568

ISBN-10: 1535582561

CONTENTS

INTRODUCTION

My name is Valiant Thor. I am a native of the interior of the planet you call Venus, where we still enjoy a finely conditioned artificial atmosphere, similar to Earth before the Great Flood.

I am on a special mission to Earth. Many Earth friends are working with us, such as the authors of this book, Gray Barker and Frank E. Stranges.

Certain security measures have been put into place, such as the use of pseudonyms, forcefields, cloaking, etc., to protect innocent witnesses and honest researchers. We apologize for these measures, but we assure you that they are essential. There are many unscrupulous individuals in the UFO field, who delight in making life miserable for seekers of truth.

We have seen the reaction to hearings in Congress and the United Nations regarding the issue of "Disclosure." We have observed an increase in the number of hoaxes in ufology. I myself have faced insurmountable obstacles in trying to get officials to listen.

Unfortunately, those in power do not currently seem interested in making life better for the majority of citizens.

Rather than give in to anger, fear, or hatred, let us move into the future together, as allies for the greater galactic good. Those with discretion, knowledge, and wisdom must make it their mission to beat back the forces of darkness and evil enveloping this planet.

We will be watching developments, hoping for the day when those involved in UFO research "vote out" their corrupt leaders and media "stars," and start afresh with the next crop of "searchers" eagerly waiting in the wings.

Embrace change, and you may just embrace truth. The very fact that you are reading this book is proof that you are open to truth.

Be prepared to launch out into exciting areas of research and investigation that will raise your consciousness as never before. Reevaluate your personal goals and seek to change them for the better. Remember, *you* must be the change you hope to see in the world.

Success and prosperity must first be experienced in the mind; then it can become reality. Remain loyal, unselfish, and loving, and devote yourself to service, charity, and commitment to God, who has chosen you for a special task. See yourself as a leader, not a follower, on the road to spiritual growth.

You are part of a plan, if you choose. Let your mind be programmed by the Divine Mind, and you will achieve great things. The decision is up to you.

Many have requested that I come and lecture, conduct classes, and teach what I know. This is quite impossible, as I must perform the following tasks in my position:

1. Command the starship as well as the Victor One Earth Module.

2. Head the Venus Council of Twelve and the Earth Council of Nine.

3. Control certain outposts around this planet.

4. Oversee taskforces used to contain radiation around your cities.

5. Make regular journeys to and from outer space.

6. Conduct seminars on the starship for briefing and debriefing of delegates visiting other star systems.

7. Monitor discussion and plans by world leaders.

8. Prevent atomic holocaust by exercising certain limits on certain human agencies.

9. Work in harmony with the Creator.

Please remember that there are, at any given time, seven humans, of varying backgrounds, who have been gifted with keen insight regarding the future of this planet.

Although Dr. Stranges and Gray Barker are no longer on this plane of existence and we miss them tremendously, their replacements also bring unique skills and understanding to solving the enigma of what you call "reality."

Dr. Ogden Pearl, the distinguished therapist who wrote the Epilogue to this book, can be trusted to relay messages to me, via Victor One, as Dr. Stranges did before his passing. It would do you good to listen to Dr. Pearl and our other six human representatives, who are making themselves known in their respective parts of the globe.

Above all, please remember to seek the good. Think thoughts of purity, godliness, and generosity. See all of humanity as one, and ignore suggestions that you should hate those who are not like you – who do not have the same skin color, religion, or status.

If you change yourself for the good, the world will also become a better place. Do not be guilty of ignorance, bias, or bigotry. Do not avoid the perfect will of God.

I leave you with my love. May God bless you and keep you through the changing times that lie ahead.

-Valiant Thor, 2016

CHAPTER 1

Stranger at the Pentagon by Dr. Frank E. Stranges
is a most interesting book. In it, Stranges explains
that since he was a true Christian, his outer space
contact, Valiant Thor, therefore seemed to use
religious or spiritual modes of expression.

One cold morning in December 1959, through
unusual circumstances, Stranges was invited to speak
with this man from another world. The meeting
took place during an evangelist crusade Stranges had
the pleasure of conducting in our nation's capitol,
Washington, D.C.

The invitation was given to Stranges by a Pentagon
official who, for obvious reasons, cannot be
named in this writing. She was, however, given a
pseudonym by Stranges: "Nancy Warren." (We will
leave it up to Stranges to reveal her true name).
Suffice to say, "Nancy Warren" is a Christian with a
sound mind and a good position at the Pentagon.

I had heard rumors that such a spaceman existed,
and that he was secretly being entertained by a few
officials in high places. I encouraged Stranges to
look into the matter, since he was the only Saucerian
correspondent with any kind of security clearance.

Indeed, Stranges was successful in passing through security, thus gaining admittance into the presence of a man from a nearby planet. The moment was not lost on Stranges:

> Since that time, I have pondered this event in my own mind, over and over again. I thought how privileged I was to have had this interview.

The great morning came. The proper arrangements had been made. Stranges was in a car, on his way to meet and speak with a visitor from the other end of our telescopes. As the car drew closer, Stranges began to formulate questions in his mind. He was ushered into the vast network of the world-famous Pentagon building in Washington, D.C.

Stranges followed the outlined plan to pass directly through the security guards.

The next thing he knew, he was standing in front of a closed door. His host instructed him to walk in and commence with the interview, and then left him standing alone.

Stranges was on his guard, having dealt with fakes and hoaxers before.

As he opened the door, he saw Army "brass" busily engaged in what appeared to be paperwork. None of these men lifted their eyes when Stranges entered the room. It was as though he did not exist, as far as they were concerned.

Then, according to Stranges, "I saw one lone man standing with his back to me, looking out a window. As I approached him, he turned slowly and looked at me. It was as though he looked straight through me."

With a warm smile, and outstretched hand, the spaceman slowly started toward Stranges:

> I felt strange all over. He had raised his hand toward me in a gesture of friendliness. As I gripped his hand, I was somewhat surprised to feel a soft texture, like that of a baby. However, his grip was that of a man – a firm grip that silently testified to strength and power.

Thor's eyes and wavy hair were brown. His complexion was unusually tan, like many of the UFO pilots and Men in Black reported by John A. Keel, Ted Owens, Jennings Randolph, Woody Derenberger, and countless other witnesses.

The very first words that fell from the spaceman's lips were, "Hello, Frank." His voice was very strong and mellow. It was filled with character and purpose, and reverberated within the concrete walls of the spartanly furnished office.

Stranges looked around the room to see whether the other men would say or do anything. They kept on about their business, as though they were not there.

During the conversation, which lasted about a half-hour, Stranges asked him many questions. He noticed that Thor was wearing the same type of clothing as he – normal. Thor stated that he had changed clothes in order to give officials a chance to run more tests on his garment.

Thor produced the one-piece garment for Stranges, which glittered in the sunlight coming in through the drapeless Pentagon windows. Thor claimed it was made of "materials not from this Earth," and that it had easily passed a fire test, an acid test, a moisture test, and had even resisted a diamond-bit drill – like a supreme form of Kevlar.

The suit contained no buttons, zippers, or snaps, and included the boots, which had been somehow glued or sewn in. Thor, however, contended that it was "held together by an invisible force."

Amazingly, Thor stated that he had come in order to help mankind "return to the Lord." According to Stranges, he spoke in positive terms, always with a smile on his face. He said God was displeased with the fact that mankind had backslidden, but that there was still a chance for us, if we would only get with the program and "evolve."

Thor stated that he had been here for three years, and was due to depart on March 16, 1960. The time of his departure was growing near, yet he felt there was still so much more to do. But his purpose would "not be fulfilled by force."

Oddly, it appeared that Thor had no fingerprints on the ends of his fingers. When questioned by Stranges on having no fingerprints, Thor stated that fingerprints "are a sign of fallen man. Fingerprints mark a man all through his life. The first thing the authorities look for at the scene of a crime is fingerprints."

Why Thor would bring up the idea of avoiding police is of interest, particularly because it indicates that he may have had some sort of spy training here on Earth.

Would someone from another planet give a hoot about our fingerprints, or our laws for that matter?

When Stranges asked him where he was from, Thor replied, "I am from the planet that is called Venus."

(Today, Stranges remains open to the idea that "Venus" may refer to a location on the astral or multidimensional plane, rather than the actual physical planet, Venus – a point often overlooked by critics and skeptics of the story. Think about it. If Thor really is on a top-level mission for his civilization – one of a truly crucial nature – he might give out the wrong location of their home base, on purpose, for security reasons.)

Stranges, a bit of a skeptic himself, asked Thor how

many others from "Venus" were here on Earth. Thor said, "There are presently 77 of us walking among you in the United States. We are constantly coming and going."

Following a discussion of life on other planets in other solar systems, Thor concluded the meeting by saying, "Please keep your faith and leave the same way that you came in. Continue to seek first the kingdom of God and his righteousness, and all other things will, in time, be added unto you and yours. Goodbye for now. God bless you and keep you always."

Stranges was moved by the meeting, and has summarized it thusly:

> As I left his presence, I still maintained a warmth in my heart. I began to wonder who would believe me if I ever repeated this strange encounter with a man from another planet. But the more I thought about it, and the more I prayed about it, the more I felt that it would bring a great blessing to those who would hear and read it.
>
> This interplanetary traveler possessed a wealth of knowledge, not only about science and about God, but also about me. He commended me on my book, *Flying Saucerama*, and stated that it

could not have been written except with Heavenly guidance. He predicted that soon, it would be read throughout the whole world. He even predicted that one day, he and I would write a book together.

Stranges has never varied on the details, much to the chagrin of his detractors. Even today, he maintains that the Valiant Thor story is entirely true. And he is apparently working on a book with Thor right now, called "Outwitting Tomorrow," which will lay out the philosophical and spiritual ideas of Thor and his space brethren.

Dr. Stranges even claims that Valiant Thor still visits Earth today. In fact, Stranges meets with him once or twice a year, at Thor's Earth module, Victor One, which is usually hidden somewhere in the Nevada desert.

Thor will never be cornered or captured again, however, because his spaceship is outfitted with high-security sensors and an invisibility shield, and his powers of teleportation have reached a much higher level since his exposure to the strong earth-energy fields of Virginia and West Virginia.

(It is reported that Thor has visited Point Pleasant, West Virginia, and may have some relationship to the spaceman there called "Indrid Cold.")

Also keep in mind that Dr. Stranges, from his days as an OSS/FBI undercover agent, knows counter-surveillance techniques. You will never be able to follow him when he goes to meet with Thor.

Besides, you might not want to know too much about this whole affair, since "knowing too much" about flying saucers is often a very hazardous business.

Many a fevered UFO buff has wandered into the domain of the demigods, only to be waylaid by the shadowy MIB, who love nothing more than to creep up to your house, late at night, after you have read a book revealing flying saucer secrets.

CHAPTER 2

Dr. Frank Stranges has a rather unique story to share. During the 1950s, he claims to have met a man from outer space, named "Valiant Thor."

This is all documented in his book "The Stranger at the Pentagon," which we have been distributing here at Saucerian for several years. In it, Dr. Stranges explains who Valiant Thor is, why he's here, and provides actual photographs proving Thor's existence.

We called Dr. Stranges recently, and asked him to recount his far-out adventures with Thor. We first asked him to provide a snapshot of himself, for our many new subscribers out there.

INTERVIEW WITH DR. FRANK E. STRANGES – *GRAY BARKER'S AUDIO NEWSLETTER* – 1983

Dr. Frank E. Stranges: I was born and raised in New York City, in Brooklyn. I went to Eastern Bible College in Valley Forge, Pennsylvania. After that, I went to North Central Seminary, which is now North Central University, in Minneapolis, Minnesota. Thanks to my dad's focus on education,

I've now managed to obtain three doctorates.

Are you still researching UFOs?

I'll be a researcher until the day I die. I love to investigate such things.

Are a lot of people skeptical about your story? One would hope that times have changed in this regard since the 1950s, 60s, and 70s. People seem to be more open-minded today.

You would think. But things are still pretty bad, especially on the university circuit. The most difficult task is to separate fact and fiction. Once you get ahold of cold hard facts, you hold onto them for dear life.

How did you meet Val Thor?

My phone rang in Irvington, New Jersey, where I lived for a short time. On the other end of the line was a gentleman by the name of August Roberts, a former U.S. Air Force photographer.

Augie was our Saucerian photography editor for many years. His disappearance was a great mystery – a deep loss for UFO research.

Yes, indeed... And he was a tireless researcher – always looking out for the next big story.

So one day, in his usual energetic style, Augie calls

and says: "Frank, I've got photographs of a man who claims to be from another planet!"

I said: "Augie, what have you been smoking?"

He said: "Now look, cut it out. This is no joke. I'm serious. I've got a picture of a man, whom I photographed in Highbridge, New Jersey, at the house of Howard Menger."

I replied: "Can you bring the photographs over here and let me look at them?"

He said: "Fine; I'll be right over." So he came over and showed me pictures of a gentleman who looked like a normal human being; yet there was something about that picture that struck me as different. I couldn't quite explain what it was.

Augie gave me that picture (of Valiant Thor), along with several others, which I have since printed in *Stranger at the Pentagon* and *Flying Saucerama*.

> *We have printed some of those same photographs in our Saucerian publications, too. So how did you come into contact with Thor directly?*

In December of 1959, I was invited to speak at a church in Washington, D.C. It was a very large congregation of several thousand people – standing room only. I spoke about UFOs and the Bible, and at the end of the meeting, a certain lady came to the platform.

She pointed to my picture of Val Thor and said: "I've got to see you privately, right now."

Well, I was bending over autographing books on the platform. I tried my best to politely refuse her, but it didn't work. She said: "I've got to see you now."

I said: "Alright, just wait a few minutes."

She then reached inside her purse and produced a Pentagon security card, and reiterated her request.

I was converted immediately. I excused myself from the platform.

Just as we left the platform, she pointed to the picture of Thor and said: "Would you like to meet him personally?"

I said: "By all means! I've been carrying his picture around with me for over a year. Where is he?"

She said: "Come into the office, and maybe I'll tell you."

Once inside, she pointed her finger at me and said, "Can you, as a former special investigator for the government, still follow orders?"

A bit shocked, I blubbered out: "Yes, Ma'am."

Again with the finger, she demanded to know: "Can you follow instructions?"

I again said, "Yes, Ma'am," though in a more determined voice.

Apparently persuaded of my allegiance, she said: "Alright, I'll take you to where he is."

"Where is he?"

"At the Pentagon. Meet me in front of the hotel at eight o'clock sharp tomorrow morning, and I'll take you to where he is."

This was really something else. I didn't sleep much that night.

I went down early, at about seven o'clock. It was a cold December morning. At eight o'clock on the dot, her car pulled up.

I got into the car, and she saluted me. I saluted her back.

Once we got there, and had gone inside (we went through a secret entrance), she flashed her photo ID, which was on the inside of her blouse jacket, several times to get us through security.

> *How did you, yourself, get through security?*
> *Did you have a temporary ID or something?*

No. It was strange. She told me to flash my jacket lapel like her, and everything would be fine. I did as she ordered, and it worked!

We turned right and went back to the corridor to

the extreme right. She said: "He's in there."

I put my hand on the door handle while she walked away, and she said something: "I'll see you in church tonight."

To which I said: "I hope so."

> *That almost sounds like a hypnotic command. Do you think she could have hypnotized you without your knowing it?*

I don't know, but it quickly dawned on me: How do I get out of this establishment?

Before I got a word out, she turned and said, "Do the same thing (open your jacket back and forth) as when you came in." I got the distinct impression that she could read my mind.

I went to the door, opened it slowly, and stuck my head inside the door. It was an office. Air Force personnel were typing away.

None of them paid any attention to me, which is highly unusual in a government office.

I cleared my throat, slammed the door, shuffled my feet, and still, no recognition whatsoever.

From my right, I saw something move. I quickly turned, and here coming toward me, with his right hand outstretched, was the man whose picture I'd been carrying around for over a year: Commander

Valiant Thor.

I asked him where he was from, and he replied, "I am from the planet that is called Venus."

I asked him how many visitors from Venus were presently on Earth, and he said, "There are presently seventy-seven of us walking among you. We are constantly coming and going.'"

How did he end up in the Pentagon?

He said he first landed his spacecraft on March 16, 1957, in Alexandria, Virginia, where he was met by two police officers, weapons drawn.

Through thought-transference, he quickly convinced them that he meant no harm, and he was ushered into the backseat of their patrol car. After crossing over into Washington, D.C., they were met by the Secretary of Defense, along with six of his staff members.

Soon police from every conceivable district and agency had joined in, all trying to claim their right to escort him to President Dwight D. Eisenhower.

Suddenly, six armed guards led Thor to what appeared to be an elevator. It went rapidly to the bottom, where maximum security was in place. After transferring to an underground train, they sped toward the White House. Six officials, six armed guards, and three Secret Service agents escorted him into the office of President Eisenhower.

Thor asked Eisenhower to visit his spacecraft, but Eisenhower respectfully declined, citing security considerations.

Soon, Vice President Richard Nixon came into the room. Nixon appeared to Val to be very sharp and quick-witted.

"My name is Valiant," he said as the Vice President thrust out his hand.

"For an out-of-towner, you have certainly caused a stir," Nixon said with a smile. "Suffice it to say, we will be checking and rechecking everything you tell us."

After assuring them that Earth has been under close scrutiny for hundreds of years, Thor was asked to follow the Secret Service back to the Pentagon. He was eventually given a beautifully furnished apartment, where he spent the next three years.

Thor, being an emissary of his people, was prepared for such a lengthy visit, and kept in constant communication with his starship. There were many occasions during which he claimed to have teleported himself in and out of those quarters.

Soon after his arrival, in April of 1957, Thor attended a UFO "convention" on Howard Menger's farm in Highbridge, New Jersey. Val and his crewmembers, Donn, Jill, and Tanyia, wore normal

Earth clothing to this event. Augie Roberts snapped several pictures, enshrining them into ufological history.

> *We published Menger's first book, "From Outer Space To You." People forget that Menger introduced the world to Valiant Thor, and that their initial meeting involved a connection to the mysterious Council of Nine Roundtable, headed by CIA scientist Andrija Puharich and Sir John Whitmore, a British medical doctor. Thor was also rumored to have been involved somehow in the notorious Philadelphia Experiment; certainly Puharich would have had an interest in the "invisibility" and "time travel" experimentation reputedly carried out there. Puharich has brought several psychics to West Virginia, because the geomagnetism there supposedly heightens their abilities. But back to Valiant Thor… Was he basically held hostage by the U.S. government?*

Not really. At his apartment, Thor was able to maintain communications with his ship, and was kept informed of world events. Plus, as I mentioned, he could slip out unnoticed whenever he wanted.

> *Self-teleportation would be a valuable skill.*

Indeed. His uniform underwent rigid tests, by the way. They attempted to penetrate the material with a diamond drillbit, but it snapped under pressure.

Acid rolled off the uniform and burned a hole in the floor.

They fired a high-velocity rifle at the uniform, but it failed to pierce it.

Is there any documentation of these tests?

Yes, and the report to President Eisenhower read:

-Physical appearance: Soft silver and gold lustrous

-Fabric: Unknown

-Weight: Six ounces total, including boots

-Style: Close fitting like a tunic – no cuffs, pockets, buttons, zippers, clips or hooks

-RXT2 Tests: Indestructible

A laser was even fired at the suit, but proved totally ineffective in damaging it.

Why do you think they chose you, Frank, to be the "contact" for Valiant Thor?

I don't know, but prior to going to Washington, D.C., I had returned from Cuba, where I had met personally with Fidel Castro.

So they wanted to "debrief" you, or otherwise check you out, after having traveled to Cuba?

Possibly. Unbeknownst to me, Val began working with "Nancy Warren" (the female agent who approached me and took me to the Pentagon) to formulate a plan whereby I would be contacted.

While in D.C., I felt that at any minute, I could be picked up, handcuffed, and thrown into some jail somewhere. My imagination was running wild. I was on my guard for fakes and frauds.

But Valiant Thor really put me at ease. His voice was very strong and mellow, filled with purpose and character.

He told me that his purpose in coming was to help mankind return to the Lord. His message was sober yet positive. He said that mankind was further away from God than ever before, but there was still hope. He told me that was going to do everything he could to help in the few months remaining before his departure.

He promised he and his people would not use force against those in authority in America; he was happy to consult with them at their invitation. He stated that thus far, only a few men in Washington knew he was temporarily residing within the Pentagon complex.

And few leaders did avail themselves of his advice, yet he felt there was still so much to do. He told me that Jesus Christ would not force men to be saved from their own mistakes.

During our thirty minutes together, he told me things about myself that even I did not know. Later, I was able to verify them with my parents and grandparents. He also gave me information that would be revealed to others over a period of years.

The only thing he said that troubled me was his use of the expression "when the time is right," in response to my question as to whether or not I would see him again.

His lack of fingerprints certainly intrigued me. I had been involved as a private investigator for quite some time, even working, at times, for government agencies.

The removal of fingerprints is a known spy tactic, so it is easy to understand why you would be concerned.

Yes, but like I said, his command of spiritual matters was formidable. I felt I had to give him a chance.

What sort of things did he say?

He told me that all Earth people had been "marked" since the fall of Adam in the Garden of Eden.

He began to prepare me for my personal journey. It would not be an easy one, he said. There would be organized attempts to both discourage and discredit me.

He was certainly right. The trials and tribulations came, but the rewards, overall, have proved to outweigh them.

He found it amusing that many theologians attempt to discredit both Jesus Christ and the Bible. The very God many have said is "dead" continues to lavish them with all good things. Perhaps they will, in time, permit the spark of Divine Light to again illuminate their troubled hearts.

In answer to my question of what he thought of Jesus Christ, he said, "I know that Jesus is the alpha and omega of your faith. Jesus Christ is the wonder of wonders, and changes not."

As he spoke these words, tears filled my eyes. He turned to the window and said, "Frank, it will not be long. Contend for the faith, and you will never miss the mark."

Did you ask him anything about science?

I asked him if there is life on other planets.

His reply was, "There is life on many other planets, of which people on Earth know nothing. There are more solar systems for which man has not even given God credit. There are many beings who have never transgressed the perfect laws of God. Mankind does not possess the right to condemn the whole of God's creation, because mankind itself has broken the perfect laws of God, through disobedience."

What did Thor think of the U.S. military?

I asked him what he would do if the military prevented him from leaving on the appointed day.

He simply smiled and stated, "Frank, do you remember the story about Jesus appearing in a locked room, in front of his followers, after his crucifixion?"

He was alluding to his ability to teleport.

Yes. And as I turned to leave the room, he said, "Please keep your faith and leave the same way that you came in. Continue to seek first the Kingdom of God, and all other things will, in time, be added to you and yours. Goodbye for now, and may God bless you and keep you always."

I left that meeting astounded, greatly encouraged, and yet with a heavy heart, not knowing what the future would hold. I began to wonder who would believe me if I ever told of this strange encounter with an interplanetary traveler possessing a wealth of knowledge, not only about science and God, but also about individual people.

Val's instructions, from Venus central command, were to leave Washington, D.C. no later than March 16, 1960. That meant that there were less than three months remaining for him to confer with scientists, politicians, and military strategists.

But they all missed his point entirely. They were filled with self-ambition, and thus cared little for the pressing needs of mankind. Thor's efforts to bring about an end to the sickness and disease plaguing this planet were ignored.

He was told over and over that his presence and his ideas were a threat to the political and economic structure. Certain religious leaders were also fearful. It was very disheartening.

Didn't he meet with President Eisenhower again?

His last meeting with the President did not reap any lasting results, unfortunately. Eisenhower wanted to let the world know of Thor's proposed plan, but the Secretary of Defense, the head of the Central Intelligence Agency, and the Joint Chiefs of Staff were opposed to his suggestion.

The President attempted to effect a joint meeting before the General Assembly of the United Nations, but this plan, too, was rejected. Most U.S. government leaders feared that if the people learned of the plan Valiant Thor was offering, they might choose to follow him instead of them.

Richard Nixon, to his credit, insisted that the President be allowed to make the choice. But he was quickly vetoed. Rigid regulations were introduced, with stiff penalties for revealing Thor's presence.

A major newscaster learned of Thor's visit, and

was silenced by none other than the Central Intelligence Agency, which has consistently disclaimed all knowledge concerning UFOs. Meanwhile, they maintain secret files that could actually prove the existence of intelligent life in the universe.

The CIA has always been more interested in the human element of ufology – tracking Soviet agents who routinely scour UFO reports for evidence of new U.S. military craft. The NSA, on the other hand, is more interested in the actual phenomenon, since it could affect their satellite communication network. Did Thor depart on schedule?

Yes. On the morning of March 15, 1960, Thor met with Nancy Warren, who would continue to work inside the Pentagon and be one of his contacts in the Washington, D.C. area. She continues to liaise with others in Thor's Earth network.

On March 16, Thor dematerialized and departed from phase one of his Earthly mission. His next stop was the outskirts of Alexandria, Virginia, where his ship and his crew awaited his arrival, hidden by a wooded area. It was no problem for the atoms in his body to reassemble inside the ship.

As his craft rose slowly, a number of people stopped and pointed excitedly. Others stood motionless, transfixed by the sight they beheld. USAF jets were scrambled, but they were unable to see Thor's ship, which has an "invisibility cloak." Even ground radar cannot see the ship.

According to news reports, there were, indeed, jets scrambled on that day.

Upon returning to his home planet, Thor attended meetings regarding the success of his mission, which had been simple:

-To mingle with and become as Earth people.

-To work and labor in Earth enterprises.

-To help those who encounter possible threat or danger while striving for world peace.

-To give them advice and guidance.

-To entrust with superior knowledge those who have proven themselves.

-To divulge the essence of their mission to the collective national leaders of Earth, but only when the time is right.

Do you not contend that Thor is still around, almost 25 years later?

Yes. As of this writing, Thor continues with this mission, assisting in preventing our "civilization" from destroying the planet. Venusians have a much longer lifespan than humans, so it is likely that we will continue to hear from Thor well into the 21st century.

There are still, to this day, many adversaries to human freedom. These parasites have imbedded themselves in all phases of human society, and will never be exposed, except by extraterrestrial intervention.

Some of these adversaries of freedom (i.e., the Nazis) perfected a saucer-type aircraft. Remnants of this group still exist, and they still want to institute a "master race." Always be wary of race-baiting and the reassembling of Nazi-friendly mega-corporations.

> *Plans for a Fourth Reich were implemented years ago, even before the war ended, and would most likely involve a saucer or drone fleet that could intervene at the height of a geophysical cataclysm, such as the shifting of the Earth's axis. Hitler was very interested in the Hollow Earth theory, and sent missions to investigate the physical and magnetic dynamics at the Poles, where the openings to the interior are located.*

Yes, the NASA photographs you printed a few years back clearly show that there are holes at the Poles. The saucers the Nazis designed are still seen in areas of South America, where they were originally built. These Nazi saucers should not be confused with spacecraft originating from other worlds.

Some have speculated that the "spaceman" Indrid Cold (above) and Valiant Thor were partners, or perhaps the same person. Cold often traveled between New Jersey and his home in Midway, West Virginia. Since this reputed photo of Cold was taken more than ten years after Thor arrived on Earth, it could be him, were he to have gained significant weight.

Cold actually bears more of a resemblance to Thor's Vice Commander, Donn, however, and could perhaps be related to him. Cold has long been suspected of having ties with mobsters in Pennsylvania and New Jersey, particularly those in the employ of Allen Dulles (suspected "father" of the ET Thesis). Following the bust-up of the Italian mob at Apalachin, New York in 1957, Dulles reputedly arranged for such mobsters to be "loaned" out to government agencies such as the FBI, CIA, and DEA.

CHAPTER 3

This is an edited transcript of a national radio interview conducted by Art Bell on his "Dreamland" program (the precursor to George Noory's "Coast to Coast AM") on October 1st, 1995. We at Saucerian feel that Gray Barker, who was friends with both Bell and Stranges, would have found this interview interesting, and so we have included it here. We ran it by Dr. Stranges before publication, and he was able to fix a few mistakes and unclear points in the transcription.

[Note to the 2016 Edition: As this volume goes to press, Art Bell remains in the hospital undergoing testing and observation. We wish him the best, and thank him for coming up with the idea for a national "paranormal" program like Coast to Coast. Under Bell's tutelage, the show became a social force in the 1990s and early 21ˢᵗ century. In 2015, it was rumored that the ever-popular Bell might again take over Coast to Coast, after a five-year absence, because of floundering ratings. But mysteriously, nothing was done. Was Coast to Coast bailed out by mysterious benefactors with deep pockets, who don't mind operating at a loss?]

Art Bell: Now, to Dr. Stranges. Dr. Stranges, are you there?

Frank E. Stranges: Yes, I'm here.

Bell: Good. Welcome to the program.

Stranges: Thank you very much. My pleasure.

Bell: I think I will start at the end and work my way back to the beginning, which I rarely do, but I would like to flat-out ask you: What, in your opinion, are UFOs?

Stranges: Well, the term itself, "unidentified flying object," speaks for itself, because "UFO" represents an unknown object, not readily identifiable as a conventional aircraft or any other aerial phenomena.

Bell: Alright. That answer would definitely qualify you for the Clinton administration.

Stranges: Thank you very much!

Bell: Assuming that they are unidentified (I will concede that point), what are they *in your opinion*?

Stranges: Let me begin at the beginning. In 1945, my research into UFOs started. I was a student at Eastern Bible College in Pennsylvania. My roommate was an ex-U.S. Marine flyer, who claimed that he saw, during WWII, three dish-shaped objects that buzzed his squadron (of which he was the commander) three times. After they had regrouped the third time, they were instructed to return the planes to the base. They were told – not asked, but told – "Gentlemen, what you saw was a flight of high-flying Canadian geese."

Bell: Ah ha!

Stranges: Well, he whipped out his pen, being a mathematician as well as a Bible student, and started figuring and calculating. He said, "Sir, the velocity, the rate of speed, the impossible right-angle turns... No sir! These were not geese!" And he was told, "Shut your mouth. Don't ever open your head about this again."

Bell: Really?

Stranges: That's right! Now, you can categorize UFOs into several different groups. Some UFOs could be figments of the imagination. Some could be secret weapons of the U.S. government. Some could be created by the Russians, using German scientists. Some of them are built in South America, by the early Nazis, and have been photographed (the prototypes were shipped from Germany). Some UFOs could be originating from the inner earth. Some UFOs could be time travelers. Some could be vehicles from outer space. Some could be entities (demonic or angelic).

Bell: I see.

Stranges: We must look at these things rationally. We should maintain an open mind, and examine and weigh all possibilities. I do firmly believe, from the depth of my soul, that "aliens" have come and abducted men, women, and children, against their will, subjecting them to all types of embarrassing situations. They're thrown on a slab and examined, probed, and poked against their will.

Bell: Don't forget the big ol' needle. They have these long needles, and the hybrid baby incubators.

Stranges: Oh yes. From my study of angelic beings and the possibility of life in outer space, I feel that these are definitely demonic. They were first to be cast out of Heaven, according to the Book of Revelation. They're part of the Lucifer entourage, the biggest counterfeiters in the business. They're trying to counterfeit everything good. Some of these UFOs may be good guys, coming here to help mankind, but these Luciferians are out to destroy mankind, by playing with our brains. It's bad.

Bell: Sort of like a Klingon saying, "I'm from the federation, here to help you." Which of the above possibilities (for UFOs) do you consider most likely?

Stranges: I believe every one of those is a strong possibility – they could, together, account for all of the UFOs visiting this planet.

Bell: Dr. Stranges, you've got an obvious religious background, and you come at it from that direction. If you were to find out that these beings were not only extraterrestrial or extradimensional, but were also actually our creators, how would your mind process that information? Now, I know it's a big "what if," but I couldn't resist asking.

Stranges: I would have a hard time accepting that because in my studies, I have looked into the Hebrew, Greek, and Aramaic languages, and I find nothing to support the "ancient astronaut" theory whatsoever. The Genesis record is quite clear. If you examine it in its entirety, in the ancient Hebrew, you'll find out that the answer is: "In the beginning, God created man," and that's it! There is something that took place between the first and second verses of Genesis 1, and I found the answer over in the Book of Jeremiah, which speaks of an entirely different civilization – of grandeur and greatness – before Adam was ever created on this planet.

Bell: A civilization on this Earth?

Stranges: Yes. A people who looked like us, and talked like us, and were just as crazy as we are.

Bell: There are a lot of people who believe that, as a matter of fact.

Stranges: Yes.

Bell: Do you not concede that those who study and

read the Bible are able to pretty much interpret it to fit what they wish to believe?

Stranges: This is what has been done in the past, but with the release of some of the information on the Dead Sea Scrolls, I've come up with a different interpretation. In the first chapter of Ezekiel, in the Aramaic language, Ezekiel attempts to explain what he saw, using the technical language of his generation. He saw a "wheel within a wheel." He said the eyes are "high and terrible." The word "eyes" can be interpreted as windows. So you've got a disc going one direction, and another one counter-clockwise. He said the thing landed, too. A portion of the Dead Sea Scrolls claim that Ezekiel walked over a "silver bridge" and into this craft. He took a seat, and looking down between his knees, saw the earth disappear in the distance.

Bell: My, my!

Stranges: We put this on videotape, and I got two calls from Israel, saying that I should be put to death for releasing such information.

Bell: I understand. There are a number of people would like me to be put to death, just for doing this program.

Stranges: I can believe that.

Bell: So this is a direct translation from the Aramaic?

Stranges: Absolutely.

Bell: From the Dead Sea Scrolls?

Stranges: Absolutely. We have made two videotapes called "The Mysteries Of The Dead Sea Scrolls." If you treat me right tonight, I may send you a copy of both of them. [laughter]

Bell: That'd be great. That would seem to argue against most traditional religious interpretations of the Bible, so it's going to make a lot of people angry.

Stranges: It will either make them angry enough to go and search the scriptures in the original language, or else accept – remain trapped by – the dogma they are studying today. I believe people have a right to know the truth. Just like in a court case, you cannot weigh things until you have all the facts. Hiding facts is wrong. I got the idea to look into this from this gentleman I met at the Pentagon back in 1957, Valiant Thor, who claimed to be from another world.

Bell: That's where the title of your book, *Stranger at the Pentagon*, came from, correct?

Stranges: Yes.

Bell: Valiant Thor was a sort of extraterrestrial "Deep Throat."

Stranges: Exactly. I was speaking at a large church in Washington, D.C. I had some pictures on a board behind me, on the platform, speaking on the subject of "UFOs in the Bible." Three particular pictures had been taken by an Air Force man, Augie Roberts, at the home of Howard Menger in Highbridge, New Jersey. Augie said that the man in the pictures could speak "every dialect and language of the wide group of people assembled at Highbridge." A lady came up behind me on the platform in D.C. and said, "I've got to see you now!" She got very irate and pulled out her Pentagon ID card.

Bell: She represented the Pentagon?

Stranges: That's right.

Stranges: We started leaving the platform. She stopped in front of the picture of this outer space gentleman, whom I found out later was Commander Valiant Thor. She asked, "How would you like to meet him personally?" Well, my God, what would *you* say? I said, "Absolutely." We made plans to meet the next morning, and she walked out the door, leaving me sitting there with my mouth open.

Bell: Wow.

Stranges: She led me through Pentagon security, after which I met with Thor for a half-hour. The following Monday, when I got off the plane in New York City, at LaGuardia, the FBI was waiting to pick me up. They asked no questions about my speaking with a man from another planet. Instead they asked, "How in the hell did you get by all those security guards without proper ID?"

Bell: Right.

Stranges: The FBI grilled me for nearly three hours. Finally, one special agent said, "Well, the guards must have been hypnotized into visualizing a badge on your shirt."

Bell: Did this spaceman, Valiant Thor, appear to be a human?

Stranges: Yes, he was 6 feet tall, and about 185 pounds. He looked from every appearance to be human. I did catch sight of his hand, however, and saw that his fingertips were as bald as a peeled egg. He had no fingerprints whatsoever. I looked at him questioningly, and he said, "You ought to know that the Bible teaches that every man on Earth is marked from the beginning, because of transgression."

Bell: Well, I'm afraid it is possible to have your fingerprints removed, is it not?

Stranges: This is true. When I worked for the Secret Service, they showed us ways you can destroy your fingerprints for a while. But they always come back.

Bell: Yes, they always come back.

Stranges: Even after using acid.

Bell: You were awarded the FBI gold medal at a police convention in Las Vegas, were you not?

Stranges: That's right. Yes.

Bell: This is a very strange story. You are living up to your last name. So you met this spaceman at the Pentagon, who claimed to come from Venus, and you had a 30-minute chat with him, correct?

Stranges: Right. And then he left here for one year. Before he left, he said to me, "I'll see you within one year." And one year from that date, I was driving up toward Beverly Hills for an appointment, at 8 o'clock in the morning, when a familiar voice rang out from the backseat. "Hello, Frank. How are you?" Well, I nearly ran a red light! I pulled over to the side of the road. He got into the front seat like a normal person, and we had a chat. We have been corresponding and meeting ever since. He has been giving me material for my books, newsletters, and videotapes.

Bell: Alright. What is the upshot, if you don't mind, of the message that he's trying to send to us through you?

Stranges: The message that we've been spreading throughout the world is the fact that mankind should learn the basic fundamental rules, like the Golden Rule, which is something that's taught in many disciplines, and by every major religion.

Bell: "Do unto others…"

Stranges: Yes. It's very, very important that we seek, in our religious work, to learn tolerance. Instead of fire and brimstone, give people something that will lift them up – that will make them have a better image of themselves. People can have faith in God, but they must also have faith in themselves, in order to accomplish things.

Bell: Here's a fax. "Dr. Stranges, there is nothing wrong in assuming that UFOs and aliens are from another planetary system, dimension, or whatever. Scripture does not say that we are alone in the universe. As you know, it indicates otherwise. The Bible is not a science book for the cosmos, but a repair manual for the human spirit. If we are in rebellion to God, why can't others in the universe be also? In other words, if Satan and his boys can corrupt us, then they can corrupt folks a few light years away, too. This explains the 'good and bad' guys amongst the visiting aliens. Remember, we are warned to look out for the 'angels of light,' who are masters of deception."

Stranges: That's true. An angel of deception is not going to validate the deity of Jesus Christ. As a matter of fact, they'll do everything they can to oppose it!

Bell: Have you seen the recent "alien autopsy" footage?

Stranges: Yes.

Bell: I would be more than interested in your

reaction to it.

Stranges: As a former special investigator, I think it was phony, from start to finish.

Bell: Well, there are certain things that we know. Some of the film was from 1947 stock. I had an FBI analyst on the show, who verified that it had to have been exposed between 1947 and 1949. It's pretty hard to buy that they would do this grand, expensive fake, way back then, and then hold onto it, just so it could be released nearly half a century later.

Stranges: I'm afraid the U.S. government has been responsible for postulating quite a few expensive fakes at taxpayer expense, in order to help prove or disprove a point. We spent a billion dollars shipping all kinds of things to a country in Africa; among that shipment were 150 thousand toilet bowls – sent to people who never used nor saw a toilet bowl in their lives. All they did with them was plant flowers in them. And we also built them an airport, complete with a control tower, even though planes never go within 400 miles of the place.

Bell: Well, we're famous for doing things like that. So, in other words, you're not surprised they would spend a lot of money to perpetrate a hoax back then, and hold onto it for whatever reason.

Stranges: No, not at all.

[Editor's note: It is also possible that someone

involved with the making of the film, say,
William L. Moore, could have gotten ahold of
some old film stock and used it to shoot new
footage. Old black-and-white negative film,
especially if kept in cold storage, can be shot
decades later and still come out fine. Anyone
who has bought old cameras at second-hand
stores – and finished shooting the rolls of film
in them – can attest to this fact. Film that has
been left in old cameras will often still work.]

Stranges: If you recall the history of the CIA, it was first known as the OSS. When Truman changed it over to the Central Intelligence Agency, the first point on their agenda was to investigate unidentified flying objects. As far back as 1938, our government was involved in UFO investigation.

Bell: Do you believe the man you met in the Pentagon came from Venus?

Stranges: Yes.

Bell: On the one hand, you seem to believe there are others elsewhere, but on the other, you seem to believe that they are mostly devils?

Stranges: Oh no. I wouldn't say that. Those that are kidnapping and abducting are the devils. But you've got countless numbers of UFO encounters, involving people from every race and every walk of life, many of whom had good meetings with these beings. They have been helped in many ways, including spontaneous healings and financial assistance.

Bell: Okay, tell us more about the good ones.

Stranges: I believe the benevolent entities can be classified as "angels" of God, or placed in the same category as Adam before the fall. I believe these beings have the ability to pass through solid matter, just like I've seen Val Thor and his crewmembers do. By the way, they are not too far from Las Vegas, Nevada tonight, aboard Victor One. They are probably listening to us right now. (Thor's saucer module is very plush. It is outfitted with the most modern, high-tech controls and appliances, and is a pleasure to board.)

Bell: Tonight?

Stranges: That's right.

Bell: Well, thanks for making me feel all the more comfortable. We're about 65 miles west of Las Vegas, out here near the *real* Dreamland, Area 51.

Stranges: I see. Their ship is parked, for your information, not too far from the shore of Lake Mead. They've been there for several years.

Bell: Let me tell you something. I got a call, prior to the show tonight, from a man in Las Vegas, who said, "Art, as the moon came up tonight, I saw no less than 48 discoid objects surrounding the moon."

Stranges: Who's to say what the man saw? Who knows his psychological profile? Who knows what trauma he may have gone through during the day? Or maybe it was a valid sighting. (Many of these sightings are seen by individuals within a group; other individuals in that same group often see nothing.)

Bell: Still, you're saying they do exist – that there are creatures from other planets, but you believe they are either 1) entities created by God, or 2) entities from the dark side.

Stranges: Yes, I believe that with all my heart. But you know, even Christ said, "In my father's house are many dwelling places… Other sheep have I that are not of this fold." We can't have a simple theological explanation for everything.

Bell: Alright. Good. Let's rock and roll. East of the Rockies, you're on the air with Dr. Stranges.

Caller: Good evening.

Bell: Hi. Where are you, sir?

Caller: Coon Rapids, Minnesota.

Stranges: That's good country. I built a church in Spring Lake Park some years ago.

Caller: Oh yes, I know where that is! My question for you, Dr. Stranges, is: Are you going to go off this planet?

Bell: Ho!

Stranges: No. I don't expect to leave here until I die. Thor made an offer to me quite some time ago in this regard, but I feel I still have work to do here.

Bell: So the offer *was* made?

Stranges: Yes.

Bell: My, my! I've often wondered about that. Now, if such an offer were to be made to me, I don't know that I would refuse. Why did you?

Stranges: Well, I have a church. I have an organization that I'm the head of. I've got a family. I've got loved ones all over the place.

Bell: Ah, that's a good answer. Were you offered a one-way trip?

Stranges: They were offering a 10-year period for me in space, but I wasn't prepared to take that.

Bell: You sound sane to me. On the other hand, a lot of the audience is probably sitting out there going "nutcase."

Stranges: That reaction is lessening as we travel through the world now, because UFOs are looked at from a much better perspective than they were years ago.

Bell: Are you familiar with the term *nanotechnology*?

Stranges: Yes.

Bell: Well, nanotechnology promises to be able to manipulate molecules through the use of tiny machines. We're on the way toward it right now. It seems to me that it may lead to the creation of new biological entities, or combinations of machines and biological beings. It's a pretty frightening prospect. If it were possible for humans, through nanotechnology, to create clones or other beings, where would that leave us?

Stranges: I think we will have violated the basic laws of God. But even if they succeed in doing that, the big question is: Will this entity have a soul? Will it have feelings?

Bell: Well, we have feelings; there's no question about that. But with regard to the soul, there is still much heated argument.

Stranges: Oh, yes. And it will continue until the end of time.

Bell: So if we created a biological humanoid, and it had feelings and emotions, and could in all ways measure up as a human being or other biological entity, we will have, in your opinion, still violated God's law.

Stranges: Yes, that's my opinion.

Bell: Alright. Back to Venus. A doctor writes that Venus is several hundred degrees Fahrenheit on the surface.

Stranges: It is more than 800 degrees at the North and South poles.

Bell: And, he says, it gets hotter as you go toward the liquid magma center, which produces the volcanoes on the surface.

Stranges: Well, to be kind to the good doctor, we are making calculations with our human technology that we've learned here on this planet. There might be some rules and regulations that apply to Venus that are not calculable by people here from Earth.

Bell: That's a good point. Alright. This is an incredible story. Can anyone else corroborate your claims? Did the stranger leave any tangible evidence behind with which Dr. Stranges can verify these events to others?

Stranges: Yes, he did. He was questioned personally, and the gentleman who did the questioning was none other than Harley Byrd, who is the nephew of the late Admiral Byrd. Harley Byrd, at that time, was in charge of the Navy department of Project Blue Book. His job was to examine the testimony of the police officers who saw the craft come down in Alexandria, and to transport Thor to the Pentagon.

Bell: You're telling me that all of this is contained in Blue Book?

Stranges: A portion of Blue Book, yes. And also in declassified CIA files.

Bell: Well, having all of this in Blue Book, how could that project have concluded that UFOs were *not* a national security risk?

Stranges: Exactly. They said they have absolutely no evidence that UFOs even exist, which runs contrary to the millions of people who have seen UFOs all over the world. Now, how they can make a statement like that and live with it, I don't know.

Bell: The crash at Socorro or Roswell was a "Mogul balloon" – that kind of thing.

Stranges: Yes. But I believe it was definitely a crash of a UFO. There's too much evidence – too many good, honest-to-God witnesses who saw something. Some of them took fragments home with them. To this day, many of them have not publicly revealed that they even have such material in their possession.

Bell: True.

Stranges: I believe there could have been dead or injured alien bodies, which were removed and brought to Wright-Patterson Air Force Base, in Ohio, for study.

Bell: East of the Rockies, you're on the air with Dr. Stranges.

Caller: The Las Vegas man who saw 48 UFOs could have seen a hologram. The human mind can be programmed to see holograms – and be programmed *by* holograms.

Bell: Could it have been a hologram, Dr. Stranges?

Stranges: Well, it could have been high-flying Canadian geese! [laughter]

Bell: Wild card line, you're on the air with Dr. Stranges.

Caller: My name is Rick. I'm calling from Madison, Wisconsin. Dr. Stranges, are you still in contact with this being from Venus?

Stranges: Yes, I am.

Caller: You mentioned earlier in the program that you had declined an opportunity to take a ride with him, away from this planet, and be part of a ten-year "exchange program."

Stranges: Yes, and I did decline. However, I have been aboard his craft on many occasions. As a matter of fact, we have meetings onboard his craft twice a year.

Bell: You do?

Stranges: Absolutely!

Bell: Biannual meetings?

Stranges: That's right.

Caller: Does this being allow other people to participate in this experience?

Stranges: He has done so in the past, yes, depending

on their background and "need to know."

Caller: Hmm. Well, I'd sure be open to something like that.

Stranges: Well, he receives many letters, every week, from people from all parts of the world, written in various foreign languages. The only thing I do is turn the letters over to him. And, thank God, he answers them himself.

Caller: I see. So I can send you some information and apply for this position, I assume.

Stranges: Why not? Other people have.

Bell: I'm curious, caller. Why would you want to go for a ten-year period?

Caller: Since I was a kid, I have taken my flashlight out in the middle of the night. I shine the light up to the stars, asking for a being to come down and talk to me. I've been interested in this for the last 20 to 25 years. I'm 30 years old, and it is something that I would definitely do. I'm not married. I have no earthly ties, if you will.

Bell: I suppose that would be one qualification in your favor.

Stranges: Well, you should drop us a letter. I'll be glad to deliver it for you.

Bell: West of the Rockies, you're on the air with Dr. Frank Stranges.

Caller: Good evening. This is Mike In Phoenix. There was a lot of talk going on a few weeks ago about the possibility that Project Blue Book was completely fictitious – that it was made up as a cover to divert people's attention away from the real facts of the Roswell Incident and other UFO incidents.

Stranges: Do you want my opinion?

Caller: Yes.

Stranges: You can put project Blue Book in the same category as the Warren Report.

Bell: Doctor Stranges, while we're at it, have you heard the talk about the Hale-Bopp comet, such as is coming from Dr. Marsden?

Stranges: Yes. I think it is very fascinating. But they forgot to mention a few things, such as that this particular heavenly body sometimes appears to be square, and sometimes appears to be round.

Bell: Where'd you get that?

Stranges: I got this from the Griffith Observatory.

Bell: Well, I do have one photograph of Hale-Bopp that appears to be a spiral. It's the damnedest thing you've ever seen!

Stranges: Yes.

Bell: But you say sometimes it appears square?

Stranges: That's right. And it has really excited some

clergy persons around the world, because they think that this could be the "coming kingdom," which is said to be "four-square."

Bell: I know.

Stranges: We'll be watching and waiting.

Bell: East of the Rockies, you're on the air with Dr. Stranges.

Caller: I imagine you know about the Zecharia Sitchin books?

Stranges: Yes, of course.

Caller: Does your theory about the Dead Sea Scrolls have anything in common with them?

Stranges: Yes, I think there's a lot in common. Those two videotapes of ours contain facts, figures, names, dates, and places of Biblical personalities who have had personal experiences with unidentified objects and with people supposedly from other worlds. That's the long and short of it.

Bell: So it actually contains detailed information, straight from the Dead Sea Scrolls, about UFOs?

Stranges: That is right. And this is why the Huntington Library in Los Angeles, the Rockefeller Foundation in Chicago, and the Institute of Biblical Studies in Jerusalem will *never* allow any of this to get out through their channels.

Bell: Most of us probably wouldn't want to accuse them of that. Have you been threatened?

Stranges: Yes. A very high-ranking rabbi said, "I'm going to have you fired from your denomination if you release this information!" I said, "Fat chance, I'm the president of it!" He hung up in my ear. The following day, he said, "You must be put to death, and the fellow who gave you this information should be put to death, because you will absolutely ruin organized religion!"

Bell: Well, you might *indeed* ruin organized religion. And that would make you a very dangerous man. Let's go back to the lines. West of the Rockies, you're on the air with Dr. Stranges.

Caller: Yes. This is Monte from Seattle, on KOMO. I have a question about interference by alien beings, perhaps long ago, which interfered with our DNA structure. Are they back here now, to reestablish our full potentials?

Bell: Can ETs interfere with our DNA structure, Dr. Stranges?

Stranges: I believe they may have tried years gone by, because every once in a while, you'll find an excavation that uncovers the skeletal structure of people who are neither animal nor human (as well as animals that are "Frankenstein" mixtures of other animals). Those could be put into that category.

Bell: Alright. Wild card line, you're on the air with Dr. Stranges.

Caller: Hi there. I'm calling from San Diego. Where in Jeremiah is there a reference to previous civilizations on Earth?

Stranges: Chapter 4.

Caller: Also, you mentioned that one of the types of beings could be of a demonic sort, and that they are the ones doing all the abductions and probing.

Stranges: Yes, those seem to be the ones that were cast out of Heaven – one third of the angels.

Caller: How do they adopt physical form and manipulate things so directly in the physical realm?

Stranges: These fallen angels and demon spirits have powers far beyond man's wildest imagination. Over many aeons, they have proven themselves to be enemies of the human race, the animals in the field, and people from outer space. Abductions, murders, and mutilations are committed by those evil spirits loosed on Earth – cast down. I don't know how we ever got so "lucky" to have them all come down here to this planet, Earth, but no other planet is mentioned in the scriptures as being the repository of demon spirits or fallen angels. The only one that has the power to leave this planet is Lucifer himself, who has free access before the throne of God. And he's continuously accusing the brethren – the people of God.

Bell: Well, it was probably that damn apple!

Stranges: It could have been.

Bell: Do you believe in entities such as ghosts?

Stranges: I believe they exist; I most certainly do. Photographers have taken pictures of ghostlike apparitions. I believe they're there.

Bell: I have such a photograph.

Stranges: You do?

Bell: I do. It is the scariest, most hair-raising thing you've ever seen! Do you use a computer?

Stranges: I'm just getting started.

Bell: If you or anyone in the audience would like pictures of ghosts and entities, they're on our web bulletin board. It is open 24 hours a day. In addition, we've got the Unabomber's Manifesto – all 37,000 words – up there for you to download. Dr. Stranges, how soon until you get a computer? You need one.

Stranges: Our church has one.

Bell: Alright. East of the Rockies, you're on the air with Dr. Stranges.

Caller: Hello, I'm in Collinsville, Illinois on SATCOM. You were discussing Hale-Bopp and maybe a biblical connection. Dr. Stranges, I'm surprised you haven't brought up Wormwood. To begin with, I talked to Sitchin and Morningstar, and it is clear that Mr. Hoagland is leaving some things out. The October issue of *Sky and Telescope* talks about Hale-Bopp looping through Sagittarius.

Stranges: Yes.

Caller: In Sitchin's "Genesis Revisited" he talks about the return of the Celestial Lord. The earliest translation talks about the Celestial Lord coming through Sagittarius. Also, regarding the swirl you mentioned in the photograph, the Hopi Indians have something that parallels it. They show a swastika spinning on a sacred tablet.

Stranges: I would recommend listeners look at *Genesis Revisited*, page 328. An ancient Babylonian text talks about how, when within the station of Jupiter, the Celestial Lord increases in brilliance. There are a lot of things that Mr. Hoagland isn't hitting.

Bell: For over ten years on this show, I have been talking about "the Quickening." It relates to social, economic, and political events, as well as with great Earth changes. We have had more hurricanes this year than in any recorded season. We've got earthquakes. We've got conspiracy rumblings. All of it seems to be converging and quickening.

Stranges: I believe that the earth itself is experiencing some tremendous changes at this time, and they are going to continue into the next century. I believe there's going to be a tremendous spiritual awakening all over the globe. And that spiritual awakening is actually going to change not only weather patterns, but also a whole host of other things.

Bell: That's quite a statement.

Stranges: Notice that I didn't say "religious" awakening; I said *spiritual* awakening.

Bell: Yes.

Stranges: In my meetings in South Korea, I've had many Buddhists in my meetings, and we've discussed some of these things about the spiritual awakening to come, which will touch practically every religion. It's going to create a newfound respect for each other.

Bell: Alright. West of the Rockies, you're on the air with Dr. Stranges. Hi. Hello there.

Caller: This is James in Oklahoma City. I am wondering if Valiant Thor has given you any information about the "faces" on Mars.

Stranges: Yes, he gave us some information. He said there is really nothing highly significant about them.

Bell: What have you learned about a previous civilization on Earth?

Stranges: As I mentioned, the first and second verses of Genesis are reflected way over in the Book of

Jeremiah. What makes this unique is that language in the fourth chapter of Jeremiah is not Jeremiah speaking, but Moses! The big question that has bothered many theologians is how in the world did that section of scripture go from the first chapter of Genesis and land way over, hundreds of years later, in the Book of Jeremiah?

Bell: What has Valiant Thor told you about this?

Stranges: He said that there was a fantastic city at one time. It rose in stature, wisdom, and understanding, to a point that no other civilization on the face of the earth has reached. But all of a sudden, something went wrong, and they met their "Waterloo."

Bell: Something went wrong because they achieved the ability to fly off of this planet?

Stranges: Yes, and they were going to take their greed and hatred – the whole imperfect gamut –with them. God would not allow that, so he shut them down.

Bell: How do we know that the Quickening will not just lead to another shutdown?

Stranges: I don't believe it's going to lead to a shutdown, because if you've taken the pulse of people all over the world, they are reaching out for something better than what they had before. They want to believe that God is a good God. He's not sitting up there with a huge horsewhip. He's here to help mankind – to help us appreciate each other's ability.

Bell: I like that. I have never thought of God as having a horsewhip myself… First-time caller line, you're on the air with Dr. Stranges. Hello.

Caller: I was wondering if you ever considered this Thor character to be the Antichrist.

Stranges: No, because he glorifies Jesus Christ and he glorifies God. The Antichrist would not, in any way, shape, or form, tell you that Jesus Christ is God, or that the word of God is true.

Bell: Very interesting. Wild card line, you're on the air with Dr. Stranges.

Caller: Does your contact from Venus ever mention anything about the human soul?

Stranges: He most certainly does. He wrote a book called *Outwitting Tomorrow*. It's in bookstores right now. In the book, he explains the makeup of the physical body, as well as the soul and spirit. He also explains the five-pointed "star of life," through which a man can perfect the above aspects evenly, so that he will be a well-balanced individual.

Caller: I'm a little bit skeptical of this great civilization idea, because although we find fossils that are millions of years old, we find nothing concrete of these civilizations.

Stranges: Well, we do have stone monuments of unusual origin around the world, which are fairly "concrete," but difficult to carbon-date. But archaeology is about putting a puzzle together. Because of the journeys ancient peoples took, you'll find mummies of those with African DNA all over the world. These people became nomads shortly after destruction of their cities, which occurred in waves due to geophysical upheavals.

Caller: So, like the Velikovsky theory…

Stranges: But it goes beyond that. For instance, if you go to Sodom and Gomorrah today, you will still find, on top of the ground, what appears to be green glass – a perfect testimony to nuclear fusion (something written about, in the Indian Vedas, as occurring thousands of years ago)!

Bell: You've done a lot of world travel. Have you ever been to Thailand?

Stranges: No.

Bell: I have, and fairly recently. In Bangkok, there is an area called Papong, where they sell little 11-year-old girls to any comer. Maybe God *should* wash the planet clean, for there is a lot of that slavery going on all over the world.

Stranges: You've got white slavery going on right here in the United States. When I worked as an undercover agent in Minnesota, Boston, and other places, we saw the exact same thing, where little kids were kidnapped off the face of the earth, often from small city parks. These kids are sold into slavery and sometimes taken to foreign countries. But I believe there's a day of reckoning coming. God is going to lower the boom on these people.

Bell: The whip will be in hand.

Stranges: Whatsoever a man soweth, so shall he reapeth. They're not going to plant corn and eat spaghetti!

Bell: Well said. West of the Rockies, you're on the air with Dr. Stranges.

Caller: I'm in Reno, listening through KOH. In your travels and information sharing, has there been anything that could give us some guidance in terms of looking after our health as humans?

Stranges: Yes. Today, there is a trend where people are looking within themselves for the first time, perhaps, and not liking what they see. The old ways are definitely looking old. The 20th century is about to give way to the 21st century, and everyone is "high" on the new computer age. They're reaching out to gather information and put that information to work – to implement that information, so that they can help themselves, their families, and their neighbors. It's an exciting time for holistic health.

Bell: East of the Rockies, you're on the air with Dr.

Stranges.

Caller: I am in Austin, Texas. Is Valiant Thor saying anything different about the purpose of life, or is he just agreeing with the Bible on everything?

Stranges: The bottom line is that he believes in what the scriptures teach.

Caller: The Bible says men shouldn't add or take away from the Word, so why do we have all these different versions of the Bible?

Stranges: You're referring to the verses in Revelation that say, "If any man adds to or takes away from the words of this prophecy, let him be accursed."

Caller: Right.

Stranges: That only talks about the Book of Revelation, not the whole Bible.

Caller: But was it really fair that we were given a heavily edited version of the Bible all those hundreds of years? Didn't the people deserve full disclosure?

Stranges: You are right. It was not fair – not at all. This is why our Dead Sea Scroll videotapes will enlighten people all over the world. There is so much information that has been withheld. The original scriptures were changed, at the very beginning. Some of them were distorted, while some of them were omitted completely, just to suit the fancy of the people in charge of the project. The 1611 King

James Version had to be completed by the King's birthday, if you will recall, which caused many errors and omissions – some by accident, some on purpose. Basically, if they hadn't finished it by the King's birthday, their heads would have rolled.

Caller: There have been recent media references to Jesus being an alien, or perhaps the Buddha. His teachings were ancient – much older than the Bible – but they were presented in a "new" way. One theory even has it that he spent his adulthood in England, where Joseph of Arimathea, his uncle, had a tin mine. There, in Cornwall, Jesus learned about the monotheism of the ancient Druids. After what could have been a 20-year-long Celtic tutelage, he took their concept of a single God back to the Middle East, where it blossomed.

Bell: Alright. We've got to hold it there. Any response, Dr. Stranges?

Stranges: Well, I don't subscribe to that at all. Jesus Christ is the Son of God. And in the Dead Sea Scrolls, he is revealed as God Incarnate.

Bell: You must run into a lot of trouble with religious folk.

Stranges: Oddly enough, only with certain religious leaders!

Bell: Do you have any knowledge about the Billy Meier affair – his contacts with the "Pleiadians?"

Stranges: I usually don't make comments about other authors or lecturers, but in this case, let me just briefly say although his UFO pictures are stunning, his story has changed quite a few times, to the point that you have to wonder what is true and what is not.

Bell: Here's a question from Fred in San Diego: "Has Valiant Thor ever revealed why there are so many different races?"

Stranges: Yes. His answer is that is the nature of the planet. We have so many species – a flamboyancy, if you will – of flowers, fruits, vegetables, people, and animals. God is a God of variety. In Sunday school, we used to sing, "Jesus loves the little children, all the little children of the world. Red, yellow, black and white, they are precious in His sight." Right?

Bell: Right.

Stranges: Well, pretty soon, as we move into a genetically modified world, we're going to have to add a few new voices. We may end up with blue or green people someday.

Bell: Oh, yes. East of the Rockies, you're on the air with Dr. Stranges.

Caller: I have a question regarding the cometlike UFOs in Pennsylvania. In one case, in broad daylight, a jet-fighter flew around the objects. Have you seen things like this?

Stranges: I have seen several UFOs. The nighttime sightings are very difficult to identify, because they could be just about anything, including experimental jets or "drones." Major Keyhoe was writing about remote-controlled airplanes in the mid-1940s, in major magazines. The technology is well known, and is built into all commercial planes today. And when you combine that with stealth technology, and the ability to spray chemtrails, you have a very powerful weapon.

Caller: This one appeared for a good 20-30 minutes during rush-hour traffic, near Harrisburg, long before the sun went down.

Stranges: We would classify that as an unidentified flying object, because we would check with the local airport and the Air Force, and find out if there were any weather balloons up at that time. If you can rule it out as a manmade object, then it goes into the unknown category – as "unidentified."

Bell: West of the Rockies, you're on the air with Dr. Stranges.

Caller: Is there any new information about the Hollow Earth theory, or Admiral Byrd's flight into the North Pole? I'm in San Francisco, on KSFO.

Stranges: Yes. I believe there is something to that theory. I have brought it up at several universities, where they have told me, in private, that they're beginning to revisit the theory, especially since they have seen the NASA pictures that show distinct openings at the North and South poles.

Bell: There's also a very interesting project going on up in Alaska, called HAARP, which has two stated goals: 1) to do ionospheric heating (to modify the ionosphere), and 2) to look for underground tunnels and caverns.

Stranges: Yes.

Bell: It's really odd. There's more there than meets the eye.

Stranges: Our satellites are able to detect openings under the ground – empty spaces that reflect radar, sonar, and microwaves differently. This stuff is still top secret.

Bell: Tell me about the photos at the poles.

Stranges: I have three NASA photographs that were taken of the North Pole by orbiting satellites. The first time around, everything was clouded over. The second time around, 50% of the cloud covering was gone. The third time around, there were no clouds, but there was an opening at the pole approximately 1500 miles across! They've been published before. I will send those to you. I just had more copies made.

Bell: Very good. East of the Rockies, you're on the air with Dr. Stranges.

Caller: Hello, this is Sky in New Orleans.

Stranges: I spoke to the Catholic University there about six months ago.

Caller: Well, I was truly deprived, then. I missed it. The things you are saying are just great. It's making people think.

Bell: Sky, do you see the same parallels that I do between Dr. Stranges and Richard Hoagland, regarding the Hale-Bopp comet?

Caller: Big time! Everything you're saying about how we should be looking inwards, spiritually, makes so much sense. And regarding nanotechnology, we don't have that right to create. And if we did create a humanoid or other organism, I don't see where they would be assigned a soul.

Stranges: No.

Caller: The only thing that they would have is their desire to survive, and that would be a problem for us!

Stranges: That's true.

Caller: How do you see things going on politically, as far as what we should focus on, or should try? Is there any credibility to the claims that our government has almost total power now to come into our lives, through surveillance and "1984" media control, and totally control us?

Bell: Let's just take the whole leap. Call it the "New World Order."

Stranges: Yes. I think that Bush and the rest are making a big mistake in espousing the New World Order.

Bell: Well, I'll vote for that. How do people get your books and videos?

Stranges: Well, they can either go down to the bookstore or they can write to me.

Bell: And, if they want to make a phone call?

Stranges: They can call NASA headquarters in Houston. Oddly enough, just three weeks ago, NASA agreed to steer all of their UFO inquiries to our office.

Bell: You're kidding!

Stranges: Isn't that something? Talk about a surprise…

Bell: No kidding… West of the Rockies, you're on the air with Dr. Stranges.

Caller: I'm calling from San Diego. Do these aliens look and speak like us humans?

Stranges: The aliens speak every language and dialect on Earth. They follow the Golden Rule more than any other single doctrine, and they ask us to examine it and practice it.

Bell: Well, I guess if everybody did follow the Golden Rule, we wouldn't have problems.

Stranges: None whatsoever.

Bell: We wouldn't even have police.

Stranges: No.

Bell: Or the FBI. Or the FDA. Or any of the other alphabet agencies.

Stranges: That's right.

Bell: West of the Rockies, you're on the air with Dr. Stranges.

Caller: This is Mack, and I'm calling from North Bend, Oregon. I didn't catch your answer as to how Venusians can live in 900-degree heat.

Stranges: Thor's people live on the inside of the planet.

Bell: East of the Rockies, you're on the air with Dr. Stranges. Where are you calling from?

Caller: Houston, Texas. I wanted to say that I think I'm in agreement with you about a third of the angels being thrown out of Heaven. My theory is that this planet is Hell. We are in Hell. We are the people who were thrown to Hell, and we are suffering in Hell right now.

Stranges: Tell that to people who are vacationing in Hawaii! [laughter]

Bell: Ha!

Stranges: Werner Von Braun was asked a question many years ago by one of our committee members: "Sir, what is your opinion of life on Earth, as opposed to life on other planets?" Von Braun stroked his chin and said, "Man would have to be an egotistical fool to think he's the only living creature in the entire universe. It is my humble opinion that the planet Earth is the *insane asylum* of the universe."

Caller: That makes sense.

Stranges: I hope he's wrong!

Bell: First time caller, you're on with Dr. Stranges.

Caller: Years ago, back in the 1960s, I started reading the Bible, and I carried it to such an extent that I kind of got the true meaning of the Bible. And since that time, God has shown me a lot of things. And one of those things is that my job, if people go too far and cross a certain line, is to release information that will cause society to fall.

Bell: That's quite a load there you've taken on!

Caller: Yes, I'm nervous right now, talking to you. I "know too much," and I don't want them to find me.

Bell: So, how are you going to do make society fall?

Caller: For about 15 years, I have written down every thought that comes into my mind.

Stranges: Hmm. You must have quite a volume.

Caller: I don't try to memorize anything. But when I get a thought, I write it down and I research it.

Bell: Yes, but, how are you going to cause society to fall?

Caller: Well, you've heard the saying "don't let the left hand know what the right hand is doing," right?

Bell: In other words, you're not going to tell us.

Caller: No, I'm telling you right now. If I'm in the center, that means I can see in all directions – like standing on a mountaintop. If I revealed the information I have – if I just rented a Xerox copier, and started copying it, and leaving it in different places – it would all be over.

Bell: Well, it will certainly be over for a few trees. With that much paper, maybe a forest or two would fall… But society? Wild card line, you're on the air with Dr. Stranges. Hello.

Caller: Dr. Stranges, have you read Graham Hancock's *Fingerprints of the Gods*?

Stranges: Yes I have.

Bell: What is your take on it?

Stranges: I believe it's a book that is well thought-out. It goes into the ancient civilization that seems to have flourished all over the world, and which worshipped a birdman deity. (That culture may have been the start of monotheistic thought, rather than the Druids, who came later.)

Bell: Do you have a final word?

Stranges: Yes. I would like to tell everybody to have faith in God. That is a must. But also have faith in yourself. Have confidence in yourself. Treat your neighbor like you would want to be treated, and look for the better things in life. Expect great and wonderful things to happen, because the doomsayers are wrong.

Bell: We do live in amazing times, do we not?

Stranges: We most certainly do. Thank you for having me. I really appreciated this time.

Bell: We'll have you back, believe me.

Stranges: Thank you.

A rare view of Valiant Thor, shot by August Roberts at Howard Menger's farm in New Jersey, 1957.

EPILOGUE

In the years leading up to the passing of Frank Stranges, I met with him many times. Given our long association over the years, and my expertise in psychology, he relayed to me several of the more harrowing adventures he had managed to get himself involved in, often through contract work with the government.

At the time, it was my opinion that he suffered from post-traumatic stress disorder, or "PTSD," most likely brought on by his Cold War activities in military intelligence.

According to declassified FBI files straight from the desk of Director J. Edgar Hoover, "The National Investigations Committee on Aerial Phenomena has corresponded with the Bureau since 1957, forwarding various material concerning flying saucers."

As many of you know, Stranges was the most active person on the NICAP staff, who did much of the PR work that established it as a national institution. Although NICAP is now defunct, aspects of it carried over to MUFON, an organization that was, believe it or not, originally co-founded by Gray Barker, under the name "The Midwest UFO Network."

In April 1962, Dr. Stranges publicly acknowledged an association with the FBI, but since then, the FBI has been unable to supply any documentation of the relationship – typical of CIs, or "confidential informants."

Dr. Stranges claimed several attempts were made on his life, and in every case, Valiant Thor (or one of his team) intervened and prevented harm from coming to Stranges.

Sometime in the 1960s, Dr. Stranges traveled to Hamburg, Germany on a mission to spread the message of Thor, who sponsored the trip. Stranges was waiting to give a lecture and went to a restaurant. Suddenly, a man came up to him gushing about his interest in Valiant Thor. The man wanted to know Thor's exact, realtime location, and seemed bent on forcing an impromptu meeting with Thor.

After saying the usual "I don't know, he contacts me only when he wants," Stranges became tired of the repetitive questions, and was about to excuse himself, when he was told by a waiter that he had a call on the house phone. When he went to answer the call, however, there was no one on the other end of the line.

Upon his return to the table, the stranger was nowhere to be seen. Dr. Stranges continued eating his tomato soup, but soon began to feel severe pain in his throat and stomach.

When his sponsor arrived to take him to the auditorium, Stranges was bleeding from the mouth, and appeared to have been poisoned. The sponsor, who was a chemist at the University of Hamburg, pulled out in packet of powder, mixed it with some water, and ordered Dr. Stranges to drink it.

Miraculously, Dr. Stranges stopped bleeding, and felt better right away.

How did the sponsor happen to have the antidote to the poison? Well, it seems that while in the lab a few hours before, he had been "moved by the spirit" to prepare a certain formula. Basically, a voice had told him the recipe and said, "You will know when to administer this formula."

The voice that the sponsor had heard turned out to be the voice of Commander Valiant Thor, who had foreseen the event and taken action, telepathically, to stop what surely would have been the murder of Dr. Stranges.

Another attempt on the life of Dr. Stranges occurred when he went to visit Thor on Victor One, which was stationed near Las Vegas at the time. At McCarran Airport, Stranges was picked up by a limousine whose occupants were – like something out of a spy movie – *impersonating* Thor's men.

Once they had driven out of town, Stranges was thrown from the vehicle, kicked to the ground from behind, and beaten by two of the men.

Within seconds, as the story goes, Commander Valiant Thor materialized, along with his Vice-Commander, Donn. To the relief and astonishment of Dr. Stranges, Thor threw the attackers several feet in the air, each with one hand, while Donn broke through the driver's window with his bare fist, pulling the stunned driver out through the broken glass (i.e., with the door still closed).

Yet another attempt was made on Dr. Stranges when he was driving outside of Las Vegas with his wife. As they were cruising down the interstate at a high rate of speed, they were blindsided by a car that appeared out of nowhere, from the side of the road.

After the accident, as doctors were running tests on him and his wife at the hospital, Dr. Stranges could not feel any part of his body below his neck. He was paralyzed.

Suddenly, Valiant Thor materialized, placed his hands on Dr. Stranges, and recited a prayer. Immediately, the good doctor stood up and walked out of the room. None of the doctors and nurses could explain the dramatic recovery of Dr. Stranges and his wife, and they were allowed to leave the same day.

Such astounding miracles are almost commonplace in the UFO community, which despite its failings, continues to draw closer to self-wisdom, through the leadership of cosmic healers like Valiant Thor.

I hope this story will encourage you to look further into the teachings of Dr. Stranges and Valiant Thor, who are loved all over the world for their warmth and kindness. Their message was free of dogma. It was spiritual, not religious.

Whether or not you believe the story of Dr. Stranges and Commander Valiant Thor, there is no doubt that the message they conveyed is one that many people in today's world find comforting and, dare I say, necessary.

-Dr. Ogden Pearl, 2016

EDITOR'S NOTE

A fascinating aspect of the strange case of Valiant Thor is that it links to other mysterious incidents of infamy, such as the Philadelphia Experiment, the Montauk Project, the Council of Nine, Mothman, Indrid Cold, and the equally strange case of Dr. M.K. Jessup, who was found dead of "suicide" during Valiant Thor's three-year stay at the Pentagon. One can even find tangential links to events like the Roswell Incident, the Maury Island Affair, the JFK assassination, Watergate and the Gemstone File, and MK-ULTRA.

(For readers wanting to explore these links, we suggest they go to Amazon and search under "Saucerian," which will give them the several hundred titles we have published over the years. In particular, Barker books like *The Ghost of the Philadelphia Experiment Returns*, *Men in Black: The Secret Terror Among Us*, *Serpents of Fire*, *Saucers of Fear*, *Saucers of Fire*, and *Time-Traveling Through Swamp Gas* should be of help.)

John A. Keel would have argued that most of these connections were drawn, concocted, or promulgated by Gray Barker, but that doesn't really explain everything. Yes, Barker made up the story that President Eisenhower met with the aliens on various military tarmacs, but Barker has little to do with, say, the beliefs of Eisenhower's granddaughter, who believes wholeheartedly in ETs and has recently promoted the Valiant Thor story, on national television, as absolute truth.

Or does he?

I myself can attest to cross connections, given that my father was present at, or possibly involved in, three of the above: the Philadelphia Experiment, the Mothman Prophecies, and the Montauk Project. As such, our family has no way of really knowing exactly why the Men in Black visited us, searched our home, or attempted to interrogate us.

We were reminded of this surveillance periodically. Whenever we drove from West Virginia to New York (where my father was from) for vacation, something weird would happen. It would usually involve an impromptu roadblock in the middle of the night, somewhere in the remote hills of Pennsylvania or western New Jersey, which would lead to my father, or us, being asked questions – possibly after being put into an artificially altered state (i.e., through drugs, hypnosis, or remote telemetry).

(I have to assume that they were making sure he wasn't taking material from his secret antigravity work at Union Carbide, and transporting it to the Big Apple. The trip took almost 24 hours in those days, on winding mountain roads; many families would rotate drivers and keep driving through the night, when traffic was sparse. Unfortunately, this made them easy fodder for the defense-industrial spooks.)

Howard Menger's farm, as well as Ivan T. Sanderson's farm – a scant 20 minutes away – were strategically located near the "Midwest" feeder routes in and out of New York. Sanderson was a "former" British intelligence agent, and Menger, during his subsequent run for public office in Florida (near where Jessup died), admitted to working with the CIA during the time Valiant Thor visited his farm.

Like many of our most famous UFO cases, the case of Valiant Thor is riddled with spooks or intelligence assets, including Thor's earthly contact, Frank Stranges, who had a long history in the shadow trade. However, I know from my own interactions with supposed ETs, MIBs, and creature entities that there is often much about them that cannot be explained away as government meddling or experimentation.

Some of it is so subtle that the government would have to be following you, and listening in, every minute of every day, which I just *don't* think was, or is, happening. The government could not be behind all the millions of strange sightings that have occurred in the U.S. Their budget isn't big enough.

I think Dr. Stranges believed everything he was saying, so it really comes down to whether or not

Valiant Thor was an alien or a human. The situation as described by Stranges could have happened, yet it also could have been faked by creative people in the intelligence community, who wanted to use Stranges to publicize a "controlled" story that might, for instance, draw out Soviet spies (who were always on the lookout for new U.S. aeronautical inventions).

I actually think both things are possible. The initial sightings of Thor could have been part of an earth-based setup, and Stranges could have had his own real encounters with the UFO phenomenon on top of that.

If you really study UFOs in depth, you run into something very unsettling; and that is the knowledge that some of them truly are unexplainable. Some actually seem organic, like they are alive. I personally think they are connected to human consciousness in some way, and will only appear under the right conditions.

Stranges clearly understood the complexity of the subject, as his interview with Art Bell suggests. This is why we should listen to him. He wasn't your average preacher, thinker, or teacher. He was truly a step above. He understood the human spirit, and was not afraid to call out those who wanted to harm others. For this he stands tall in the history of ufology.

-Andy Colvin, 2016

Valiant Thor (right) and his sub-commander, Donn, at Howard Menger's farm in 1957.

Thor (right), was often accompanied by his second-in-command, Donn (center), and his lovely secretary, Jill (left).

Jill (left), Donn (center), and Thor (right) listen intently to the world problems discussed at Menger's UFO convention in High Bridge, New Jersey.

Thor (right) took notes during the meeting, and vowed to help the people of Earth save their civilization and planet. The lady to whom he gave his seat (second from right) has never been identified.

A close-up of the dapper Thor, who reportedly was a riveting and convincing speaker.

Printed in Great Britain
by Amazon